D1568839

THE BEAUTY OF
BONSAI

THE BEAUTY OF
BONSAI

A GUIDE TO DISPLAYING AND VIEWING NATURE'S EXQUISITE SCULPTURE

The names of modern and contemporary Japanese appear in Western order, while those of
historical figures (pre-1868) are written in traditional order: surname preceding given name.

Layout by Yuki Harasawa

Edited in cooperation with Musashi Editorial Ltd. and Matt Cotterill

Special thanks to Uhaku Sudo

Photos courtesy of Shunkaen Bonsai Museum, Reiji Takagi, Sagami Shohin Bonsai Society,
Shofu Shohin Bonsai Society and All Japan Shohin-Bonsai Association Shugaten Executive
Committee

Distributed in the United States by Kodansha America LLC, and in the United
Kingdom and continental Europe by Kodansha Europe Ltd.

Published by Kodansha International Ltd., 17-14 Otowa 1-chome, Bunkyo-ku,
Tokyo 112-8652

ISBN 978-4-7700-3126-6

First edition, 2010
18 17 16 15 14 13 12 11 10   10 9 8 7 6 5 4 3 2 1

Library of Congress Cataloging-in-Publication Data

Yamamoto, Junsun.
  The beauty of bonsai : a guide to displaying and viewing nature's exquisite
sculpture / Junsun Yamamoto ; preface by Masahiko Kimura ; translated by
Kirsten McIvor ; photography by Shigeru Masuda. -- 1st ed.
       p. cm.
  Includes index.
  ISBN 978-4-7700-3126-6
  1. Bonsai. I. Title.
  SB433.5.Y36 2010
  635.9'772--dc22
                     2010023114

www.kodansha-intl.com

CONTENTS

Sargent juniper: Toryunomai (*Dance of the climbing dragon*)

P R E F A C E

Long in years and lashed by the elements, yet surviving against all odds; scaled-down scenes of mighty trees thriving in the most severe of environments—this is bonsai. Even one's first encounter with bonsai can conjure up rousing images. Study that tree intently and summon your powers of imagination, and I guarantee you will perceive a landscape extending far beyond it, and feel profoundly inspired.

One of the arts most symbolic of Japan, bonsai imparts a profound sense of seasonal beauty. It is a cultural treasure that cultivates a peaceful outlook on life, and sets the soul at ease. A love of both nature and of peace is essential for raising bonsai, and I have no doubt that bonsai can help us build a more peaceful world. Thus I hope people everywhere will learn to appreciate the magic of bonsai and through bonsai nurture their own desire for peace.

The main purpose of this book is to explain a few basic principles that will enhance your appreciation of bonsai. From the following pages you will learn the right way to view a bonsai, and understand its creator's intention. And should this spark a real interest in bonsai, by all means seek out the genuine article and extend your explorations of this ancient art. Lavish affection on a tree as its grows, care for it properly, and you too will experience the delight of raising a bonsai that with each passing day looks more like that landscape visualized in your mind's eye. Then yours will be a bonsai soul, a soul of peace.

My latest passion is creative bonsai—recreating majestic landscapes in pots. My aspiration is to produce a totally new kind of bonsai, taking inspiration from the natural world to create works of art with a different look, a different ambience to classical, conventional bonsai.

Masahiko Kimura
BONSAI ARTIST

INTRODUCTION

In Japan, there are certain persistent stereotypes associated with bonsai. One is that of an old man on a veranda carefully snipping branches of his bonsai, lost in reverie. A ball then flies into the garden, crashing into the bonsai on the shelf and breaking a branch, prompting the old man to emerge and angrily lecture the errant child. Another common image is one of rows of stately bonsai artfully arranged in spacious grounds, with a tycoon-like figure strolling among them, hands clasped behind his back and deep in thought. Thus in Japan at least, tending to bonsai is often perceived as a hobby for retirees with money and time on their hands. A stereotype not wholly without foundation, but in reality reflecting only one facet of this time-honored pursuit. There is infinitely more to bonsai than this picture suggests.

As a hobby, bonsai does indeed have a great deal to offer elderly people with time to spare, and the wealthy. Those with abundant leisure time can water a tree four or five times a day in midsummer, while those with abundant cash can purchase a prized 300-year-old specimen for their own pleasure. But there are many bonsai enthusiasts without the luxury of leisure time who find ways to grow excellent bonsai with only morning and evening watering. And there are many on modest incomes who take great pleasure in nurturing a bonsai over thirty years from a seed or cutting. Thus there are no constraints to pursuing this splendid art.

You can even make bonsai your hobby without owning a single tree, instead finding delight in the outstanding efforts of others. This costs very little, and most importantly, you need never worry about a tree dying. Simply head to a bonsai exhibition and admire bonsai grown, shaped, and displayed perfectly—what could be easier?

Of course, like most other arts, true appreciation of bonsai requires mastering a few tricks first. Doing so will elevate your understanding of bonsai to a different plane altogether.

Japanese zelkova

This book uses photographs of a variety of bonsai displays (known as *sekika-zari*) to explain in simple terms all anyone needs to know to get the most out of viewing bonsai. Even if you know nothing about bonsai, these pages will provide a thorough grounding in the main points. With a little imagination you will cultivate the ability to view trees in a "bonsai fashion." And when it comes to not only looking at the trees but actually growing them, knowing the correct way to view bonsai will make a tremendous difference to how your skills progress. When you know the right way to look at a bonsai will you be able to grow good bonsai. Technique comes later, with time. Learning how to truly appreciate bonsai may even inspire you to visit Japan's largest bonsai exhibition, the Kokufu Bonsai-ten held each year at the Metropolitan Art Museum in Ueno Park, Tokyo. Let your bonsai journey begin!

Junsun Yamamoto
AUTHOR

Flowering quince: Chojubai

Getting to know bonsai

Bonsai as Landscape Painting

A Japanese bonsai expert once opined that a potted plant is a work of horticulture that lets us enjoy the beauty of foliage and flowers, but a bonsai is a work of art that lets us savor the beauty of trees and plants in the natural landscape, expressed in a container. This sums up the major difference between an ordinary potted plant and a bonsai: bonsai have an added scenic element. The container provides the setting for a particular vista or landscape. Bonsai is more than a quest for beauty in form; it is a spiritual, artistic realm in itself that presents an imaginary landscape to show how a particular tree grows, and in what environment.

Take the Japanese black pine (*kuromatsu*). Black pines growing near the coast are battered by high winds, and often have slanted trunks. Alternatively, a pine may sprout from a seed in a small hollow of a cliff face, roots wound tightly around the rocks, launching itself into midair. Such environments are far from favorable, but the sight of trees doggedly surviving the most severe conditions can be truly inspirational. Some of us may attempt to capture the scene in a photograph. Those skilled in drawing may reproduce it in a sketch. A bonsai artist will take a single black pine tree and use it to create a landscape painting in a pot.

Never make the mistake of thinking that bonsai takes natural beauty and confines it in a small container. In fact the reverse is true. The aim of bonsai is to take a single tree and from it construct a majestic landscape where there was nothing. A landscape not confined by photographic paper or sketchbook, but extending into infinity. A bonsai that presents such a vision is a superior bonsai indeed.

The moon behind a plum tree. Viewing from other angles may alter the scene significantly.

Shohaku bonsai

From weathered bark to twisted trunks, *shohaku* bonsai (evergreen conifers) never fail to fascinate. Perennial favorites over the centuries, they still account for the majority of bonsai. Typical species: Japanese white pine, Japanese black pine, Japanese red pine, Sargent juniper, Japanese yew, needle juniper, Japanese cedar, Japanese cypress.

Japanese red pine

Hamono bonsai

From spring buds through the vivid greening of summer, scarlet and gold tints of fall, and stark sculptural shapes of winter, *hamono* (literally "leafy") bonsai are transformed by the seasons. Typical species: zelkova, *momiji* maples, *kaede* maples, cherry, Siebold's beech, star jasmine, willow, *himeshara* (orange-bark *Stewartia*), Japanese wax tree, ivy.

Himeshara

Hanamono bonsai

These are trees at their finest when in bloom. Achieving the right balance between tree and flowers is paramount: no blooms and the bonsai will look a little forlorn, too many and it will be scruffy and inelegant. Typical species: Japanese apricot (*ume*), cherry, *satsuki* azalea, forsythia, flowering quince, crape myrtle, spike winterhazel, wisteria.

Yellow star jasmine (*Trachelospermum asiaticum*)

Mimono bonsai

Bonsai cultivated for their appearance when in fruit. Look for branches adorned with colorful fall berries: examples include the scarlet of *ume-modoki* (*Ilex serrata*), the orange of princess persimmon (*Diospyros rhombifolia*), and the pink of spindle tree. Typical species: *ume-modoki*, Chinese quince, spindle, winfed spindle (*Euonymus alatus*), firethorn (*Pyracantha angustifolia*), Japanese beauty-berry (*Callicarpa japonica*), Rock cotoneaster (*Cotoneaster horizontalis*).

Persimmon

Bonsai Have a "Front"

All bonsai have a "front" view, further testament to their affinity with paintings. They are designed to be appreciated from a particular angle, and this is the main feature that distinguishes bonsai from other forms of planting.

Ordinary potted plants do of course have an angle most suitable for viewing, but generally this is the side that displays the flowers or leaves to best advantage, and is not fixed. Bonsai, however, have an obvious front view that remains unaltered at least until the next repotting. Not surprisingly, great care is taken when determining which side of a bonsai will be the front.

So on what is that decision based? On the elements that determine the value of a bonsai, such as visible roots (*nebari*), distribution of the branches (*edaburi*), and tapering of the trunk (*kokejun*). These and other characteristics emblematic of bonsai will be explained in more detail later; for the moment suffice it to say that they are all taken into account when choosing the side of the tree that will be the front, that is, the side that in future will display the tree to the greatest advantage.

But of course trees have a life of their own, regardless of human designs, which makes it difficult to achieve anything near the ideal form. From time to time a vital branch is sure to wither and die, and a more suitable angle for the front view may present itself. This is why bonsai growers choose the best front each time they repot, assembling a new ideal vision of the tree in their mind. This is also one of the most enjoyable aspects of growing bonsai.

Hollow in a Japanese white pine. Hollows like this that add tremendous character are another deciding factor when it comes to choosing a front view. That they are not seen as a fault is yet another fascinating aspect of bonsai.

Japanese white pine

Nebari (visible root base)

Sturdy roots extending vigorously across the surface of the soil are one of the most attractive features of bonsai. *Nebari* with roots of no obvious difference in thickness, extending uniformly in all directions, are known as *happone*, literally "roots in eight directions," and represent the classic *nebari* aesthetic. In contrast, roots that are entwined or reach over others are called *imine* (undesirable roots) and not favored by bonsai enthusiasts. Generally the side of the tree that feels most stable, with roots extending to left and right, is chosen as the front.

Kaede maple

Edaburi (branch distribution)

In the classic bonsai form, branches grow from the bottom of the tree upward, alternating left and right, with the back branches stretching out behind adding depth, and the gap between branches decreasing toward the apex. In terms of branch length, the *ichi-no-eda*, or lowest branch, tends to be long, with branches shortening as they approach the top, the aim being to reproduce the look of a large tree in nature.

Chinese quince

Kokejun (tapering)

Kokejun refers to a gradual tapering of the trunk and of individual branches. This is achieved artificially over time by repeated growing and cutting of the trunk and branches. A skilled bonsai grower will concentrate any cuts to the trunk and branches at the rear of the tree to make them invisible from the front wherever possible. As one might imagine, a bonsai with inferior *kokejun*, that is a trunk or branches the same thickness at top and bottom, will not resemble a tree in nature.

Japanese white pine

Olden is Golden

In the bonsai world, age (*jidai*) is revered. Put simply, *jidai* means "of ancient appearance." Take the rough, scratchy bark of a black pine, the rounded *mizusui* ("waterline" or living part of the trunk) of a juniper, the withered, hollowed-out trunk of a wild *ume* (Japanese apricot), or the smooth golden skin running to the tip of an orange-bark *Stewartia* branch where the delicate bark has peeled off. The more features such as these—only found in very old trees in nature—the higher a bonsai will rate among enthusiasts and experts. It is an aesthetic preference peculiar to bonsai. At bonsai exhibitions, no tree younger than about twenty years will be accorded any genuine value, even if it has been grown and shaped to look like a large tree. This is because while it's possible with the aid of fertilizer and water to make a tree grow a thick trunk and branches, and through techniques such as wiring to make it look old, a true appearance of *jidai* will remain elusive. And with daily watering the destiny of the bonsai

enthusiast, raising a tree successfully to a ripe old age is a true challenge.

An age-old Japanese veneration of ancient trees lies behind this desire to reproduce them in bonsai. Mighty trees in the grounds of shrines are deemed sacred, generations of worshippers admiring their ability to survive the disasters and destruction of centuries. Inspired by a tree's stoic longevity, they join their palms in a prayer for similar good fortune. For the Japanese, old trees are like gods, to be revered.

The age of this Japanese apricot is manifested in its battered bark.

Japanese apricot

II

Viewing bonsai

Sargent juniper

Japanese white pine

Creating a Landscape in a Display

Cultivating bonsai is tremendous fun. Naturally there will be the occasional setback—a tree killed by disease or felled by strong winds, or a precious branch broken. But patiently nurturing a bonsai and watching it begin to resemble a venerable old tree is what bonsai growers love best. Most bonsai hobbyists will be content simply to raise such a tree, but bonsai's greatest satisfaction lies one step beyond, in displaying the tree indoors to be viewed and appreciated.

Bonsai are trees originally found in the wild and deliberately cultivated in compact form for indoor display, but while they are being grown outdoors they cannot be described as bonsai. Only when a tree is complete, combined with a suitable container, displayed in the *tokonoma* (alcove) at the right time of year, and viewed by others does it truly become a bonsai. Needless to say, simply placing a bonsai in the *tokonoma* does not constitute a bonsai display. The host (*sekishu*) arranges the bonsai in the style of a majestic landscape painting.

This is achieved with the aid of props such as accent plants, *suiseki* (natural stones thought to resemble natural features, such as mountains) viewing stones, scrolls, and tiny models or ornaments known as *tenpai*. These props possess specific meanings in terms of such variables as season, climate, location, and time of day, and positioned effectively will vividly evoke the envisaged landscape. Too overtly representative and they will look childish, but anything too abstract is also to be avoided. The *sekishu*'s vision of a landscape is one thing, but the choice of a single prop of this sort can speak volumes about his or her aesthetic sensibilities. If you are invited to a bonsai display, take a good look at the components presented to divine what sort of landscape the *sekishu* has created by specifying elements such as season and location.

Bonsai are displayed on a type of stand known as a *shoku*. *Shoku* are broadly divided into tall and horizontal types, fundamentally for different tree shapes. For a tree in cascading style, growing as if projecting from a cliff face, a tall stand would be chosen to emphasize the image of a sheer drop, while low horizontal stands tend to be employed for bonsai in informal and formal upright styles.

Deciphering Bonsai Displays: Alcoves

Keido, founded in 1986, is Japan's leading school of orthodox bonsai display. Keido's object is to popularize bonsai appreciation by constructing elegant, well-balanced displays dividing items such as trees, containers, stands, ornaments, and scrolls into the calligraphy categories of *shin*, *gyo*, and *so*, that is, formal, semi-formal, and informal, and combining elements of the same category. The following are some examples of the basic classifications.

Among tree species, evergreens are *shin*, shrubs *gyo*, and grasses *so*. Among tree shapes, tidy, well-proportioned bonsai such as formal upright (*chokkan*) and informal upright (*moyogi*) trees with thick trunks constitute *shin*, and thinner trunks *moyogi*, while trees with slanting trunks are *gyo*. Cascading trees, group plantings, and *bunjin*, or literati-style bonsai, are classified as *so*. In pots, unglazed earthenware such as *udei* and *shidei* are *shin*, glazed pots are *gyo*, and coarser items such as the shallow dishes referred to as *nanban-zara* are *so*. In terms of pot shape, generally speaking oblong containers are *shin*, oval and square *gyo*, and round *so*.

Take a look at this *tokonoma* display (*tokokazari*) assembled by Uhaku Sudo, second-generation head of the Keido school. The location is a ten-mat room at Jigyotei Wakian, the Keido teaching facility. It's a sweeping landscape; a luxuriant black pine with a natural feel set against the backdrop of magnificent Mt. Fuji. *Ajania pacifica* as the accent plant tells us that this is a seaside setting. Turn your attention to the ornaments to the right, and you'll find the figures of an elderly couple. These indicate that the theme for this display is *Takasago*, one of the most famous plays in the Noh repertoire. Expressing the hope that a couple will remain close companions forever, their relationship flourishing like the evergreen pine, this makes the perfect display for a celebration such as a silver or golden wedding anniversary.

TITLE	Takasago
TREE	Japanese black pine: Hagoromo
AGE APPROX.	300 years
POT	*Kowatari hakudei* (white clay pot imported prior to 1568)
SCROLL	*Fugaku-zu*. Depiction of Mt. Fuji by Gejo Keikoku
ACCENT PLANT	*Ajania pacifica*
ORNAMENT	Takasago, by Kano Tessai

Different Ornament—Different Story

Mr. Sudo then replaced the Takasago figures with the figure of an elderly priest. Now we have the medieval poet and priest Saigyo looking up at Mt. Fuji from the pine-covered beauty spot of Miho-no-Matsubara. Saigyo gazing at Mt. Fuji is a time-honored subject in Japanese painting.

TITLE Saigyo gazing up at Mt. Fuji

ORNAMENT Saigyo figure (wood). Edo period (1600–1868).

Deciphering Bonsai Displays: *Sekikazari*

For a *ryurei* tea ceremony (i.e., using a table and chairs) arranged to permit guest movement in and out of the venue, the most suitable bonsai display will be a relatively informal one, perhaps a *mimono* bonsai, *hanamono* bonsai, or *kusamono* bonsai. Or, if a pine tree, perhaps something in literati style.

Mr. Sudo chose a chrysanthemum. Not just any chrysanthemum however, but one almost finished flowering, pinpointing the season at around late fall. The scroll in the background is a hazy rendering of maple trees on a lakeshore. The faded maple, no doubt about to scatter its leaves into the lake, and the chrysanthemum mustering the last of its strength for those final few blooms, complement each other perfectly. Sudo dubbed this display Nagori (Remnants).

Display at a *ryurei* tea ceremony venue with an earthern floor.

A switch in scroll

Sudo then swapped the scroll for one depicting deer, by Murase Soseki. The scene is early winter, when the maple has lost its leaves. Unable to find food, one surmises, the deer cries piteously next to a clump of withered *susuki* grass.

As a backdrop this scroll throws into even sharper relief the forlorn quality of the last chrysanthemum flowers. The ability to thus change location by switching a single ornament, and mark the passage of time by switching a single scroll, is what makes bonsai display so fascinating.

Maple by Kawabata Gyosho

Deer by Murase Soseki

Ultimate Bonsai Settings: Reimeian

The single-story building known as Reimeian is a structure of great historical significance in bonsai. Reimeian was originally a teahouse built for bonsai viewing by Kyuzo Murata, bonsai grower and founder of the Kyuka-en nursery in the bonsai growing district of Bonsai-cho (Saitama City). Painstakingly constructed by Murata with the aid of a skilled carpenter, building of Reimeian began in 1932 and was completed five years later in 1937.

Post-war Prime Minister Shigeru Yoshida is said to have sought spiritual solace here, visiting Kyuka-en

Interior view of Reimeian; a bonsai venue assembled without a single nail, using only saw, plane, and chisel. The scroll in the center is the work of the late Sobin Yamada, a priest of the Daitokuji Shinjuan temple in Kyoto.

Reimeian entrance. Murata formed the name Reimei by taking a character each from the name of the late Reiji Takagi, director of the Takagi Bonsai Museum, and the name of his company Meiko Shokai.

A fragmented semicircular window, assembled entirely from bamboo.

and this teahouse surrounded by bonsai for a contemplative interlude between his public duties. From the 1930s through to the post-war years, many bonsai lovers found their way to this building until, with the downsizing of Kyuka-en, it was dismantled and put into storage. Then in 2000, to coincide with the relocation nearby of the Takagi Bonsai Museum from Tokyo's Ichigaya district, it was restored to its original state for bonsai fans to enjoy once again.

Despite the extraordinary pains taken by Murata to investigate the right wood to use, the design, and the proper construction techniques for the teahouse—a meticulous obsession with detail that meant it took a full five years to complete—there is nothing remotely flashy about Reimeian. Elegant and refined, it sits unobtrusively in its grounds, a true reflection of the personality of its creator, legendary bonsai grower Murata.

A teahouse is an enclosed space where the host serves tea and chats with invited guests, rendering it largely inaccessible to anyone without an invitation. But not this building. Its design makes it difficult to tell where inside ends and outside begins, making for extraordinary ease of entry and exit. This deliberate accessibility creates a very pleasant ambience.

TITLE   Kohan no aki (Fall on the lakeshore)
TREE   Japanese white pine (from the Kishu Tokugawa clan)
SCROLL   *Geese at sunset* by Tosa Mitsuzane
ORNAMENT   Three-tiered pagoda (wood)

At Reimeian, the distance between bonsai and viewer is perfect. Seen from the raised area, the tree is at an angle. Thus to contemplate the tree straight on, one must view it from a half-sitting position, while on the earth floor of the teahouse. This may seem somewhat inconsiderate of Murata, but he probably wanted to avoid forcing visitors unfamiliar with bonsai to adopt a formal kneeling position (*seiza*) in front of the tree. To me this is quintessential Murata: the idea that if people want to look at a tree, they should do so at their own leisure. Not that Murata was downplaying the importance of display. Proof of this is the absence of a central pillar in the building. The pillar has been omitted to allow an unimpeded view of the bonsai display from anywhere in the building, and even from the garden, through massive glass doors. Seven decades later, Murata's bonsai philosophy lives on in the subtle details of this intimate teahouse.

Tosa Mitsuzane was a painter of the late Edo period. This scroll depicts the early fall scene of migrating geese prior to landing at the water's edge.

The paper window showcases the pagoda to optimum effect.

45

Ultimate Bonsai Settings: The Waiting Shelter

Between viewing one bonsai display at the teahouse and proceeding to another, the guest stops a while at the waiting shelter, or *koshikake machiai*, to sit and contemplate the garden, or perhaps a special stone on display. If viewing bonsai can be likened to a banquet, this is a palate cleanser between courses. Displays in such settings tend to be of a more casual style, employing stones, grasses, and suchlike.

Inside the shelter

A famous "sky dragon stone" suggesting a white cloud in the shape of a dragon passing over a mountaintop.

Exterior view of the shelter in the outer tea garden, with the ground covered in cedar moss.

Garden with beautiful fall tints viewed from the shelter.

A First-Hand Experience of Keido Hospitality

Jikyotei Wakian was built in the *sukiya* (teahouse) style by renowned master *sukiya* craftsman Sotoji Nakamura. At this Keido learning facility for the study of bonsai display, second-generation Keido master Uhaku Sudo presents formal bonsai displays. The author paid a visit to experience the art of Keido hospitality.

1. Sweeping

The host personally sweeps the path in preparation for the guest's arrival.

2. Uchimizu

He then sprinkles water at the entrance, a custom known as *uchimizu*. In winter this is performed an hour before the guest's arrival; in summer thirty minutes before; and during the hottest part of summer, fifteen minutes ahead of the scheduled arrival time.

3. The visit

Everyday attire is perfectly acceptable, but male guests should wear a necktie.

4. Welcome

The guest is welcomed at the entrance. The host will greet any guests of higher status than himself at the gate. On formal occasions he wears a kimono bearing his family crest.

5. Ushering in

Leading the guest, the host opens the door of the room, and bows.

6. Greeting

Host and guest exchange seasonal greetings before turning to the subject of the bonsai display in the *tokonoma*.

7. Explanation

The first display is of the *setsugekka* variety featuring snow, moon, and flowers, with an *ume* as the main tree. After spending some time viewing the scene depicted in the display, the guest offers his impressions. If requested, the host will explain the display.

8. Main display in the *ohiroma*

After strolling in the garden and viewing a *suiseki* display in the waiting shelter, the guest is invited into a larger drawing room (*ohiroma*). Here he first bows toward the *tokonoma*, a custom arising from the belief that the ancestors of this household and other revered spirits reside there.

9. Viewing

After bowing in the direction of the *tokonoma*, the guest bows also to the host. A formal kneeling (*seiza*) position is preferred for viewing.

10. Main display

A 300-year-old Japanese white pine in *moyogi* (informal upright) style, passed down through the Kishu branch of the Tokugawa clan. The pot is an oval container with a rim, a perfect complement to the tree's robust trunk. The scroll is the work of Tsunayoshi, the fifth Tokugawa shogun.

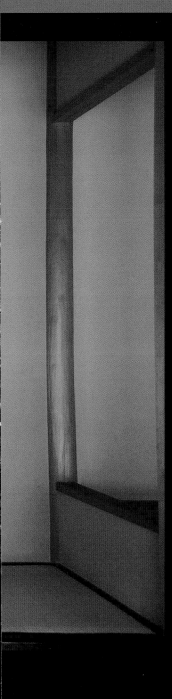

11. Scroll

Reputedly painted by Tsunayoshi in his thirties. A solitary heron, feeding at water's edge in midwinter when the lotus flowers have died off, is rendered in delicate brushstrokes, the image a reflection perhaps of Tsunayoshi's solemn commitment to affairs of state even in the most turbulent of times.

12. Viewing

Having obtained the host's permission, the guest may view the display at closer quarters. After completing this study of the display, he offers his impressions.

13. Service

Once the host has served up sustenance for the eyes and soul through the bonsai displays, his wife serves the guest tea and cakes.

14. Soko Sudo, a tutor at Urasenke, the leading school of Japanese tea ceremony, in action.

15. The guest drinks the tea then expresses his gratitude to the host and his wife for their hospitality.

Scene with water pitcher, watering can and *shohin* bonsai.

CHAPTER **III**

Fun with *shohin* bonsai

Sargent juniper

A Quest for the Small and Perfectly Formed

Tiny bonsai that fit in one hand are known as *shohin* bonsai. These measure roughly 10–20cm in height; trees of less than 10cm are referred to separately as *mame* bonsai.

Shohin bonsai are a popular choice among Japanese, due to their cute and compact forms, or more practically, to the lack of space in people's homes. Young women otherwise unfamiliar with bonsai often display a *shohin* bonsai in their apartment as an alternative to cut flowers, the idea being to add a touch of traditional Japanese aesthetics to their living space. But don't think the no-fuss image of *shohin* bonsai means they are easily mastered. The minimal quantity of soil in the pot means that in high summer even one day of watering missed can kill a *shohin* bonsai, and if exposed continuously to cold winds in winter, the soil will freeze, destroying any hope of healthy budding in spring. Growing one of these tiny trees can be unexpectedly challenging. Which of course only makes a *shohin* bonsai carefully nurtured over several years all the more impressive.

The compact dimensions of *shohin* bonsai mean that in terms of natural ambience they will inevitably be inferior to ordinary bonsai. As if to compensate, they surpass ordinary bonsai in forming interesting shapes that make the most of a tree's unique character. We may contemplate a thick-trunked *moyogi sho-hin* bonsai and struggle to recall a similar tree anywhere in nature, but still feel drawn to its seductive beauty. Learning to appreciate the singularly weird and wonderful shapes of *shohin* bonsai is part of the pleasure of these quirky trees.

A *mame* bonsai maple measuring just 4cm

Moyogi (informal upright style)

Moyogi are trees with a trunk tracing a natural curve upwards to the left or right, forward or backward. *Moyo* means a pattern, and in bonsai refers to this curve of the tree trunk. The ideal *moyogi* has loose roots that taper toward the tips, with branches attached to the outer edge of the curving trunk.

Japanese black pine

Chokkan (formal upright style)

Trees in the *chokkan* style have a trunk extending perpendicularly from root to apex, in the style of a Japanese cedar. The ideal *chokkan* bonsai has sturdy roots spreading in all directions, and tapers gradually toward the top from a stable root base.

Japanese cedar (*Cryptomeria japonica*)

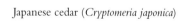

Shakan (slanting style)

Shakan trees are those that have grown at an angle. This may be caused for example by exposure to a prevailing wind, or the presence of an obstacle such as a rock. Thick, sturdy roots extend in the opposite direction to the sloping trunk, clinging to the ground and giving the tree a sense of stability.

Nioi kaede (perfumed maple/*Premna japonica*)

Sokan (twin-trunk style)

Sokan bonsai are trees with two side-by-side trunks of different sizes growing up from the roots. The taller, thicker trunk is known as the *shukan* (main trunk), and the thinner, shorter trunk the *fukukan* (auxiliary trunk). The feature to look for in *sokan* trees is a perfect balance between *shukan* and *fukukan*.

Fossilized cypress

Kabudachi (multiple-trunk style)

In *kabudachi* bonsai, five or more trunks grow from a single root. The rule since early times has been to have an odd number of trunks, e.g. five, seven, or nine, the logic being that an even number of trunks is artificial, but adding an extra one gives the tree a more natural aura.

Ume-modoki (*Ilex serrata*)

Hokidachi (broom style)

Hokidachi bonsai have a trunk extending straight up from the roots that is replaced by branches partway up as if torn apart, these branches developing still finer twigs. Resembling an upside-down broom (*hoki*), the form is found occasionally in zelkovas, and appears to best advantage when the delicate branches are exposed in winter.

Zelkova

Kengai (cascade style)

The term *kengai* is used for trees that take root in steep cliff faces, such as coastal cliffs or gullies. They are typically battered and warped by wind, and grow with their trunks drooping. Any tree designed to have the tip of a branch lower than the edge of the container is classed as a cascade bonsai, while that with the tip above the bottom of the container referred to as a *han-kengai* or semi-cascade tree.

Japanese black pine

Bunjingi (literati style)

Originally the favored style of scholars and poets, lovers of calligraphy and painting, antiques, poems, and songs, the ideal *bunjingi* possesses a thin trunk akin to that of a red pine at the roadside, just a few branches, and rough bark for a weathered, aged appearance.

Japanese red pine

Neagari (exposed-root style)

Neagari bonsai mimic the trees spotted occasionally on hillsides where soil has been gouged out by the elements or a landslide, exposing the underground roots, which then continue to grow above ground. These trees are prized for the artistic effect of entwined roots of different thicknesses.

Spindle tree

Ishizuki (rock-grown style)

A tree planted in, for example, *keto-tsuchi* soil in the hollow of a stone to represent a particular landscape: perhaps a valley or coastal scene. Over many years tree and rock merge until eventually the creator's work is no longer discernible, and the tree becomes a genuine *ishizuki* bonsai.

Kaede maple

Shohin Bonsai Display: *Sekikazari*

Like larger bonsai, finished *shohin* bonsai are displayed indoors. The designated space for a *sekikazari* display of *shohin* bonsai is roughly the area of a single tatami mat—180cm wide and 90cm deep.

Ordinary *sekikazari* of three components employ a main tree known as the *shuboku;* a second counterbalancing tree, or *uke,* that receives the "flow" of the main tree and anchors the display, and an accent plant. Displays of two components are simpler, containing just a single bonsai and accent.

In both cases, the accent plant can be swapped for an ornament or *suiseki* stone, depending on the scene. When assembling the display it is important to ensure pots are wiped before placing on a low or high stand, or a *jiita* (flat board), for presentation in clean, tidy condition.

High stands, associated with topographical features such as precipices and valleys, are used for *kengai* bonsai; low stands or tables intended to resemble hills for the likes of *moyogi,* *chokkan,* and *shakan* bonsai; and boards, which suggest flat land, for *bunjingi* bonsai and accent plants.

A two-piece arrangement of red pine and lion-dance ornament to celebrate New Year.

MAIN TREE
Sargent juniper

ACCENT
Kogane-shida (*Woodsia macrochlaena Mett. ex Kuhn*)

HANEDASHI (OUTER TREE)
Ume-modoki (Japanese winterberry)

Shohin Bonsai Display: *Hakokazari*

Sekikazari displays on racks are known as *hakokazari* or *tanakazari*, literally, box or shelf displays. In the Meiji period (1868–1912) when cultured, literati-like pursuits were all the rage, people displayed antiques, *suiseki* stones, and other such treasures in their homes, and the racks they used provide the prototype for those used in the display of *shohin* bonsai.

Timbers used for racks include rosewood, ebony, and Chinese quince. Lacquer-coated racks are the most highly prized. The top level is known as the *tenba*, and is used for displaying a sturdy main tree, generally an evergreen of some kind. The *chudan*, or middle tier, is for shrubs, and the *gedan*, or bottom shelf, for shrubs or grasses with a lighter, more airy quality. Care is taken with the flow (orientation) of the trees to direct the eye naturally from top to middle to bottom, and to ensure that the different elements of the display are not cramped. As a rule the same species of tree is not used more than once in any single display.

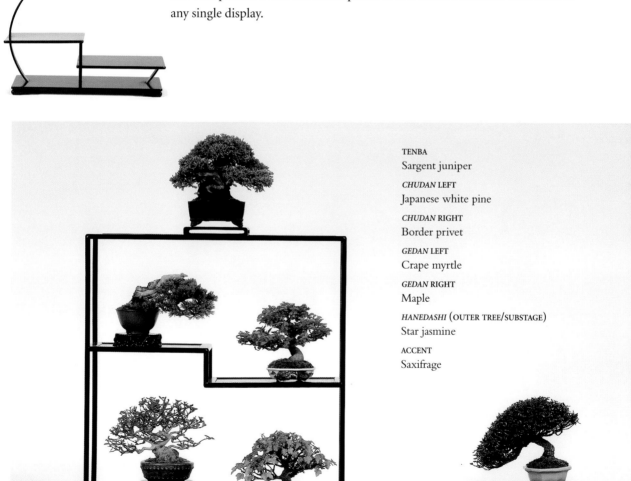

TENBA
Sargent juniper

CHUDAN LEFT
Japanese white pine

CHUDAN RIGHT
Border privet

GEDAN LEFT
Crape myrtle

GEDAN RIGHT
Maple

HANEDASHI (OUTER TREE/SUBSTAGE)
Star jasmine

ACCENT
Saxifrage

Props Adding Color to Bonsai Displays

Props or ornaments, known as *tenpai*, are indispensable to bonsai display. *Tenpai* are used to endow the scene depicted with a more tangible quality: perhaps positioned next to a bonsai to reinforce the image of a large tree, indicate a specific location, or add a seasonal touch. The addition of a single ornament can supply an entire narrative, so the ornaments come in many different types, with many different themes.

Typical examples include wild birds such as cranes, wagtails, and sparrows; small creatures such as frogs and crabs; Buddhist images such as of Kannon (the Goddess of Mercy) and Jizo (Ksitigarbha); and structures such as five-tiered pagodas and bridges. The materials used are just as diverse, ranging from ceramics to metals to wood.

Another common component of *sekikazari* displays is the *suiseki* stone, resembling a natural feature such as a waterfall. One particularly popular *suiseki* is the *kuzuya-ishi* stone, resembling a thatched house in a mountain village.

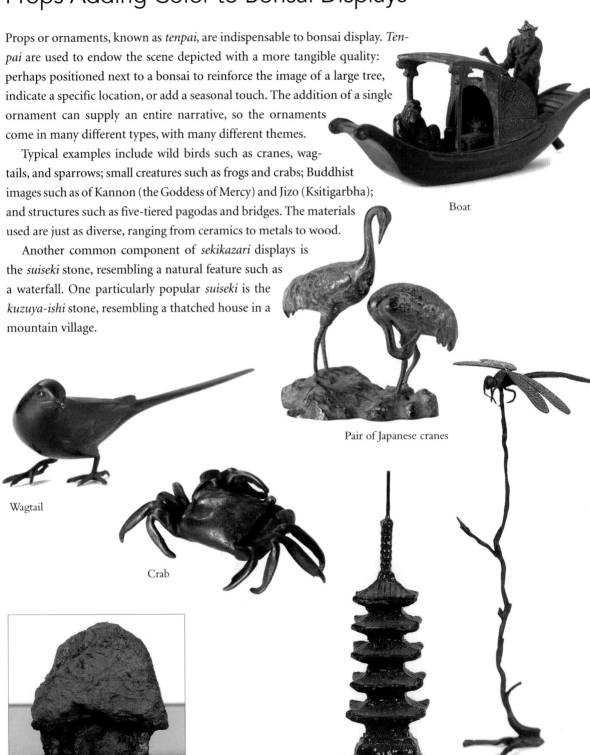

Boat

Pair of Japanese cranes

Wagtail

Crab

Thatched house

Five-tiered pagoda

Dragonfly

The Distinctive Delights of *Shohin* Bonsai Pots

MAKUZU KOZAN II

Round yellow-glazed pot with protruding rim and *kirin* (the most powerful of Japan's mythological creatures) pattern

As above, back view. For convenience this was designated the back, but there are three illustrations, any of which could be at the front, according to taste.

As above, backstamp. The signature of the maker is enscribed on the base of the pot.

The "bon" of bonsai refers to the pot, and the "sai" to the tree. Thus it is the harmonious combination of container and tree that constitutes a bonsai. It follows that even the most magnificent specimen will seem no more than a simple nursery tree if planted in a second-rate pot. A bonsai only becomes so when placed in a vessel befitting the grace and dignity of the tree, and which shows off these and the tree's other attractive qualities to greatest advantage. The task of finding the perfect pot for a particular tree is known as *hachiawase*, literally, pot matching. One of the bonsai enthusiast's many pleasures, it is also a task to be approached with caution, because a well-chosen (or ill-chosen) pot can dramatically alter how a bonsai is perceived. Successful *hachiawase* results in a bonsai celebrated for its good *hachiutsuri*, or pot harmony. *Hachiutsuri* is of particular importance in *shohin* bonsai, because they are viewed at a closer range than larger bonsai.

Bonsai containers can be broadly divided into unglazed and glazed pots. Unglazed pots, or *deimono*, are high-fired without the application of glaze, and come in several types depending on the color of the clay, including brick red *shudei*, dark brown *udei*, purple clay *shidei*, and *hakudei* white clay pots. These are the pots of choice for trees such as Japanese white pine, black pine, and juniper. Colorful glazed pots with ornate patterns tend to be used for shrubs and accent plants. Choosing a pot to highlight the color of flowers or fruit is one of the delights of *hachiawase*. Many a bonsai connoisseur has been more charmed by the beauty of a container than its contents, and has decided to give up cultivating trees and concentrate instead on collecting *shohin* pots. You will no doubt understand why after perusing the famous pots featured here, dating from the Meiji through to the early years of the Showa (1926–89) period, that is, before World War II.

Heian Tofukuji

Heian Tofukuji (1890–1970) made the bonsai pots that are most sought in Japan today. Tofukuji never had his own kiln, instead firing a variety of pots at a rented climbing kiln in Kyoto. The popularity of his containers is due not only to their beauty, but also their ability to display trees to greatest effect. A prolific potter in his time, even today—almost forty years after his death—Tofukuji's work continues to grow in value and reputation.

Rectangular pot with green glaze and cord effect

Rectangular pot with lapis lazuli glaze
and wood-fire effect

Rectangular pot with frame effect and pearskin finish

Jun ware rectangular pot with rounded corners and rivet
pattern

Round hand-formed yohen pot

Heian Kozan

Master bonsai pot maker born in 1905 and often ranked alongside Heian Tofu-kuji. Many of his pieces are relatively delicate for Japanese bonsai containers, and his style, typified by sleek lines without the slightest warping, earned him the appellation Kamisori (Razor) Kozan. He later changed his potter's name from Kozan to Kohou.

Rectangular pot with colored illustration of the Eight Sages

Rectangular high-fired unglazed pot with plover design in gold and silver

Rectangular pot with colored flower and vine design

Rectangular "chicken blood" glaze pot

Rectangular pot decorated with a scene from the famous animal caricature scroll *Choju-jinbutsu-giga* (National Treasure, credited to Toba Sojo)

Takemoto Hayata

Artist (b. 1845) who dedicated himself to the study of bonsai pots while bearing witness to his country's modernization, from the upheaval of the late shogunate to the Meiji Restoration (1868). Takemoto played a pioneering role in the study of glazes, and his pots in subtle hues achieved using a variety of glazes have earned him a legion of fans, not only among *shohin* bonsai enthusiasts.

Octagonal *mado-e* (window picture) pot

Geho-bachi (slightly tapered pot)

Square white porcelain pot with crackle glaze

Rectangular green-glazed pot with protruding rim

Thread-pattern pot with red copper glaze

Yusen Tsukinowa

Born in 1902, this inspired maker of illustrated *shohin* bonsai pots was origi-nally a specialist painter of high-end Shimizu-yaki porcelain, and only began producing bonsai pots in his fifties. Most of his pieces were in porcelain, their delicate yet vibrant designs on a white background exerting a huge influence on the illustration work of later ceramic artists. Containers with *mawashi-e* (a picture running around all four sides) are quintessential Yusen.

Sometsuke blue and white landscape painting

Sometsuke blue and white landscape with brown rim

Red overglaze pot with foliated rim

Oval pot in five colors with dragon motif

Rectangular yellow-glazed pot with rounded corners and window pictures

Makuzu Kozan

The first Makuzu Kozan was born in 1842 and opened a kiln in Yokohama in 1871. Although ranked as one of the three greatest craftsmen of the Meiji era, he made only a few bonsai containers. It was his second son, Makuzu Kozan II, who produced most of the bonsai pots, including the famous work on p. 69.

Fukuro-shiki (sack–style) oval pot with bright green glaze and daybreak motif

Inoue Ryosai

The name Inoue Ryosai encompasses three generations of renowned potters that first emerged in the closing years of the shogunate. Both the first and second Inoue bequeathed to the bonsai world some exquisite pots, but most of the bonsai containers attributed to the name are the work of Inoue Ryosai III, born in 1888. His round pot with a *soba* (buckwheat) glaze and floral crest motif, a superb example of wax-resist technique, is an inspired piece of truly distinctive character.

Round three-legged pot with black glaze and floral crest motif

Dainihon Kanzan

Born in 1821, he earned an international reputation in the early Meiji years as a producer of ceramics for export. While he made only a handful of bonsai pots, these deep square and rectangular specimens are highly artistic in their depictions of landscapes, birds, flowers, and other motifs from nature, thanks to Kanzan's consummate command of Western pigments.

Rectangular decorated white porcelain pot

Eiraku Zengoro

The Eirakus are a renowned family of Kyo-yaki potters engaged for the past seventeen generations chiefly in the production of tea ceremony utensils. Excursions into bonsai pots are rare, although famous specimens produced by members of the family such as Hozen (b. 1795) and Wazen (b. 1823) do remain, as well as these pots by Eiraku Zengoro.

Hexagonal pots with indigo and yellow glaze

Ono Gishin

Ono Gishin (b. 1839) forged successful careers in government administration and finance during the early to middle Meiji period. Constructing the Ono kiln in his backyard, he summoned renowned ceramicist Kato Shokichi from Owari (Nagoya) and produced a stream of pots. Ono's work is typified by round pots with an *adzuki* or green glaze, molded on a turntable, but very few examples are extant.

Kawaribachi joined pots

Takahashi Dohachi I

One of a family of ceramic artists from a Kyo-yaki kiln in business for eight generations and still going strong. Since the late Edo period the kiln has produced many well-known *sencha* tea cups.

Blue porcelain pot in *mokko* scallop design

Seifu Yohei

Seifu Yohei was a renowned name in Kyo-yaki ware for five generations. Almost all bonsai containers bearing the name are the work of Seifu Yohei V, who also made pots in collaboration with Yusen Tsukinowa.

Hexagonal pot with red design

Tosui Uematsu

Tosui pots are deemed to be those designed by Uematsu Chotaro (b. 1901), son of a family of pot sellers, and produced by Seto potter brothers Harumatsu and Masao Mizuno.

Rectangular pot with runaway-horse design and pearskin finish

Chazan Asai

Born in 1904, he is known for his illustrations and etchings on Tosui pots, specializing in designs featuring hermits, flowers and birds, and dragons.

High-fired unglazed *kawaribachi* pot with hermit illustrations

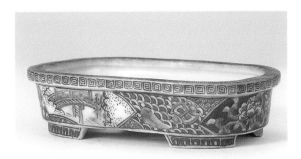

Oval pot with red design

Taizan Koito

Taizan Koito (b. 1911) produced a mere 200 or so bonsai pots, all in a short but productive burst soon after World War II. Most were small porcelain pieces, identical in shape but with individual designs.

Rectangular pot with *soba* (buckwheat) glaze

Ichiyo Sanshu

In the pre-war years when Chinese bonsai pots were all the rage, Ichiyo Sanshu (b. 1902) traveled to potteries around Japan, devoting himself to the study and development of original Japanese pots. After the war he used this knowledge to instruct young up-and-coming ceramicists, while producing his own small pots.

Square pot with colored illustration

Kakiemon Sakaida

The name Kakiemon has been associated with Imari-ware for fourteen generations, dating back to the early Edo period. Kakiemon pots are elegant pieces featuring paintings of birds and flowers on a soft white porcelain background, and making clever use of blank space. This pot is the work of Kakiemon Sakaida XIV (b. 1934).

The creative bonsai of Masahiko Kimura

Sargent juniper: Toryunomai (Dance of
the climbing dragon)

Mountain gorges visited by Kimura on a trip to China are the inspiration
for this creative bonsai. First he recalls the scene in a painting.

What Is Creative Bonsai?

No one beats Masahiko Kimura when it comes to finding the perfect way to present a bonsai at its finest. No matter how unpromising the tree, give it to Kimura and once he has worked his magic it will come back almost miraculously improved. It's hardly surprising then that in the leadup to major shows like the Kokufu Bonsai Exhibition, there is barely room to move in the Kimura garden for all the bonsai entrusted to him by growers across Japan.

Kimura's style is not so much natural as sculptural; bonsai with a logic and consistency to the very tips of their branches. For this reason his work has occasionally been dismissed as overly artificial, because Kimura persists in producing bonsai all too obviously shaped by human hands, when the most venerated specimens are those betraying no trace of human intervention.

But on actually encountering a Kimura creation closeup, one discerns a magical, indefinable landscape looming in the background, and suddenly questions of natural or artificial are no longer of consequence. Here simply stands a Kimura bonsai, utterly convincing in its own right.

The tools used by Kimura for sculpting stone.

Despite his status as a giant of the ancient and at times impenetrable world of bonsai, Kimura stands out for his inexhaustible sense of fun. Nowhere is this playfulness more obvious than in the creative *ishizuki* bonsai he has been producing since the 1990s.

To make his bonsai Kimura takes a piece of Kurama-ishi granite that would normally be laid horizontally, and stands it upright, cuts it into pieces with a chainsaw, and stacks and arranges the pieces to form a base on which he plants juniper, cypress, and other seedlings he has carefully raised himself. In doing so, Kimura experiments with creative bonsai in totally new ways and in a deceptively effortless fashion, in the process producing scenes of rare beauty and originality. A display of just one of Kimura's creative bonsai suggests a majestic, intriguing landscape instantly recognizable even to a child. No need for statues, scrolls, or accent plants: it is just pure genius.

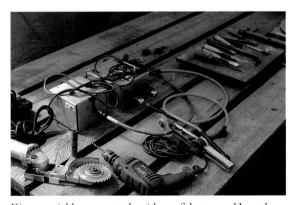

Kimura wields power tools with confident ease. He makes many of his own tools, guarding them from inquisitive eyes.

1. A large chunk of Kurama-ishi granite.

2–3. Using a power saw of his own design, bonsai master Masahiko Kimura cuts into the stone.

4–6. Working with two apprentices—each member of the team knows exactly what to do.

7. Kimura performs the most vital cutting personally.

8–9. The stone now ready for sculpting

SCULPTING

10. Taking a power saw to the cut stone, Kimura begins sculpting.

11–12. Observing Kimura's movements, an apprentice applies chisel to stone.

13. The stone starts to resemble a mountain, albeit vaguely.

14. Kimura places the trees for planting against the stone to see how they look.

15. Finishing the stone.

16. The fine details are chiselled by hand.

17. Large sections of carving are performed by power saw.

18. The completed base stone.

PLANTING

19. Cypress trees cultivated from cuttings for this *ishizuki* bonsai

20. After exposure to the elements for a month or so, wires are attached to the stone to hold the trees in place.

21–26. Now to make the envisaged landscape reality. From here on the job is Kimura's entirely. The roots of the seedlings are placed in the central hollows, and *keto-tsuchi* soil is pressed firmly on to hold them in place.

27. Finally, moss is added for a natural touch.

Japanese Cypress: *Ishizuki* A is now complete. Take another look at the painting on p. 86 and see how they compare.

THE COMPLETED TREE

A Selection of Creative Bonsai

Japanese cypress: *Yoseue*

Sargent juniper: *Ishizuki* A

Sargent juniper: *Ishizuki* B

Sargent juniper: *Ishizuki* C

Japanese cypress: *Ishizuki* B

Parts of a Bonsai

a Trunk height—the height of the tree from roots to apex. Height may also be used to classify bonsai: trees with a *juko* (height) of over approximately 60cm are classed as *omono* (large) bonsai, those between about 25 and 60cm as *chuhin* (mid-size) bonsai, those under around 25cm as *shohin* (small) bonsai, and those under 10cm as *mame* (miniature) bonsai.

b Tapering—from the base of the trunk up to the top. Achieved skilfully, it makes the bonsai look like a tree in nature, and/or have the proportions of a large tree. See p. 25.

c Branches are referred to as *ichi-no-eda, ni-no-eda* (literally, first branch, second branch) from the soil surface upward. In good *edaburi*, the branches extend from the trunk alternately left and right in a well-balanced manner, the interval between branches narrowing toward the top of the tree, and branches reducing in length. See p. 24.

d Base of the tree. Preferably stable roots that grasp the soil firmly. See p. 24.

e Term used for the qualities that characterize any particular leaf, such as shape, size, or color. Conifers should preferably have thick, straight needles, while in shrubs, small leaves that provide a good display of fall tints are said to have good *hasho*. The smaller the leaves, the closer the bonsai will resemble a large tree, so dwarf (in Japanese, *yatsubusa-sho*) varieties which have even smaller leaves than usual are especially popular.

f A part of the trunk or a branch that has died off and bleached white due to abrasion, breaking, etc. In bonsai a dead trunk is referred to as a *shari*, and a dead branch as a *jin*. *Shari* and *jin* can be produced deliberately to add appeal, by carving into the living trunk.

g The "bon" of bonsai refers to the pot, or *hachi*, the most important element in determining the allure of a tree. The antique look of the pot, and other aspects of its appearance, must complement the tree. See p. 69.

h Special stand used in the display of bonsai. See pp. 32-33.

b *Kokejun*

a *Juko*

d *Nebari*

c *Edaburi*

Maple

e *Hasho*

f *Jin/Shari*

g *Hachi*

h *Shoku*

Sargent juniper

Flow and Counterbalance in *Sekikazari* Displays

Flow, or *nagare*, refers to the direction in which a tree is aligned—to right or left—when viewed from the front. It is one of the basic concepts of bonsai. Trees of cascade and slanting *shakan* style have an obvious flow, while in *chokkan* and *kabudachi* style bonsai for example, the flow is very subtle.

When two or more bonsai are displayed together, a tree is placed as a counterbalance (*uke*) to the main tree, accepting its flow, the display arranged so that the trees highlight each other's best qualities. Displays with a good relationship between flow and counterbalance have an air of stability; those with a poor relationship can seem unsettled, lacking calm. In the following examples the relationship between flow and counterbalance is shown using arrows, to help readers understand the concept intuitively.

Display of two items

flow

counterbalance

A

B

The subtle flow of (A) a Chinese persimmon (*Diospyros rhombifolia*) is gently balanced by (B) an accent plant.

Display of three items

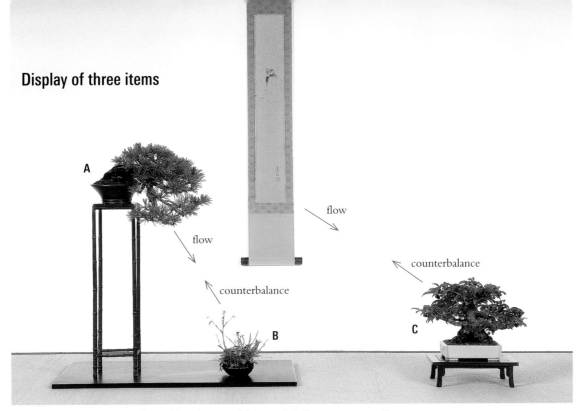

The main tree (A) is a cascading white pine on a high stand. It flows on to a small accent plant (B). The tree (C) placed slightly apart from the others is referred to as the *hanedashi*, and always plays a counterbalancing role. A pine (A) has a pronounced flow, so a sturdy *mimono* tree (C) provides the perfect balance.

Display of five items

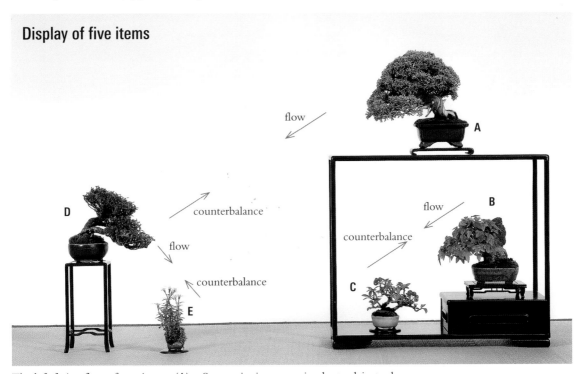

The left-facing flow of a main tree (A), a Sargent juniper on a simple stand, is steadfastly balanced by the pronounced flow to the right of a *hanedashi* shrub (D). On the bottom shelf (B) and (C), and in the *hanedashi* (D) and (E), also form flow and counterbalance relationships.

Display of six items

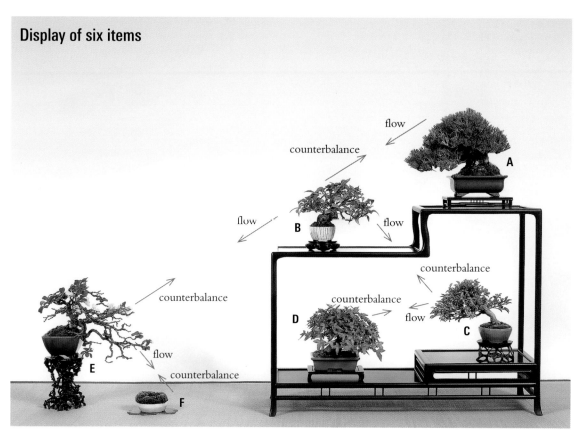

In a display of six or more items, the eye first takes in the plants from (A) to (B) to (C) to (D), then moves to *hanedashi* (E) and (F). Thus it is important to arrange flow and counterbalance so as not to interrupt this line of sight. The left-flow of the black pine (A) that is the main tree is countered by the right-flowing (B), while the right flow of (B) is balanced by the left flow of (C), and softened by (D) with its subtle right flow. The left-facing flow of the stand overall is balanced by *hanedashi* (E), with the right flow of (E) quietly balanced by the moss (F). The eventual balancing of a magnificent pine (A) by the tiny moss (F) gives this display such a rare and exquisite quality.

G L O S S A R Y

Arakawa-sho: Condition in which a tree has rougher bark than others of the same species, giving it an aged feel even when young.

Araki: Tree taken from the wild, on which no work has yet been done. Also referred to as *genboku*. Trees grown from cuttings or seeds are known as *naegi* or *tanegi*.

Atama: The "head," or top of the tree. Also referred to as the crown.

Baiyo: Raising a tree, making a bonsai.

Bunjingi: Tree form with fine branches, no lower branches, and only sparse branches and foliage.

Chokkan: Bonsai style inspired by the straight-growing cedar, forming a largely symmetrical, triangular shape with the trunk in the center. Ideally the tree will have roots that extend firmly in all directions, and a trunk with a sturdy base, tapering gradually toward the top.

Deimono: Ceramic pot fired without glaze.

Eda-uchi: The way in which the branches form on a tree and extend from it; for example the interval between branches, their thickness, length, and configuration. Also known as *eda-jun*.

Eda wo nuku: To remove a branch at its base. In bonsai the term "remove" (*nuku*) is preferred to "cut."

Fukinagashi: Bonsai style modeled on a tree whose trunk and branches lean in one direction due to lashing by wind.

Futeiga: Superfluous bud that has sprouted where a branch would be pointless.

Giseishi: Branch grown without cutting for a certain period to make the trunk wider, then removed.

Hachiage: Moving a tree or grass, raised in the ground or from a seedling, or a cutting into a pot for the first time.

Hachiawase: The task of finding the best pot for a particular tree.

Hachiutsuri: Harmony of pot and bonsai.

Hachi wo yurumeru: Literally, "loosening the pot." Repotting a bonsai in a larger container.

Hamono: Non-*shohaku* bonsai cultivated for their seasonal changes in foliage. From new spring growth through the vivid greening of summer, beautiful fall tints, and stark winter shapes, the ever-changing foliage of *hamono* bonsai offer an alluring taste of the seasons.

Hanamono: *Zoki* trees cultivated for their appearance in bloom. The attraction of *hanamono* lies in their flowers, but achieving proper balance with the tree is vital. A tree with too many blooms will look unkempt; too few, a little forlorn. In bonsai the greatest admiration is reserved for trees with just the right floral coverage.

Harigane-kake: Wrapping a tree in copper or aluminum wire to bend the trunk or branch/es into the desired shape.

Hasami-zukuri: Shaping a tree without wiring, just pruning.

Hasho: Properties that distinguish a particular leaf, such as thickness, shape, and color. In coniferous trees, "good *hasho*" refers to needles that are on the thick side—straight, short, and vibrantly colored. In *zoki* it refers to small, shiny leaves, and leaves that turn vibrantly colored in the fall.

Hokidachi: Tree form resembling an upside-down broom (*hoki*). Used for zelkova. The trunk grows straight up from the roots, splitting into branches partway up as if ripped asunder, with these branches in turn developing finer twigs, and the branch tips, tracing a semi-circle.

Ichi-no-eda: Closest branch to the roots. Bottom branch.

Imieda: Branch that detracts from a bonsai's appearance, making it unsuitable for display.

Imine: Root that detracts from a bonsai's appearance, making it unsuitable for display.

Ishizuki: Bonsai style in which the tree is planted in the hollows of a distinctive stone rather than a traditional pot, using *keto-tsuchi* soil, or a suitable equivalent. The roots are carefully trained to cling to the stone, resulting over time in a perfect fusion of tree and stone.

Jidai: Age, or a feeling of age. The phrase "*jidai ga notteiru*," i.e., to "have good *jidai*," is used in reference to the likes of old trees and well-loved pots. One of the elements by which bonsai are judged.

Jiita: Wooden baseboard used for bonsai display.

Jin: See "*shari*."

Joryokuju: General term for evergreen trees.

Jukaku: A bonsai's "quality of character." If the tree is cultivated correctly, this will grow with each passing year.

Jusei: Describes the health and growth of a tree. If a tree is said to have good *jusei* it is strong and dynamic.

Kabudachi: Bonsai style in which multiple trunks extend from a single root. An orthodox *kabudachi* consists of a relatively thick, tall main trunk and several smaller trunks of varying height and girth.

Kaerumata: Literally, "frog's legs." Trunk or branches forked in a wide U-shape. Classed as an *imieda*.

Kaisaku: To alter the form of a bonsai significantly.

Kanju: A deciduous tree that has lost all its leaves, leaving just trunk and branches. Also called a *raju* ("naked tree").

Kannuki-eda: Type of *imieda* in which two branches grow left and right out of the same part of the trunk, resulting in an undesirable "V" shape.

Kanseiju: Bonsai completed and refined to a state fit for viewing.

Kansho-bachi: High-quality pot that is suitable for bonsai display and heightens the appeal of the tree. Also known as a *hon-bachi* or *kesho-bachi*.

Kasanari-eda: Type of *imieda* in which closely-spaced branches extend in the same direction.

Katanebari: Type of *imine* in which too many roots extend in the same direction.

Katte: Flow or orientation of a tree on display. A *hidari-katte* flows from left to right, a *migi-katte* from right to left.

Kawa-sho: Properties of the trunk surface.

Kazari: Bonsai display.

Kengai: Bonsai modeled on a tree clinging tenaciously to life in a small cliff hollow, its trunk and branches battered and bent by the elements. When the tips of the branches extend below the base of the pot this cascading style is referred to as *kengai*; when above the base of the pot it is referred to as *han-kengai*, or semi-*kengai*.

Kiki-eda: Branch that is a stand-out feature of the tree as a whole.

Kokejun: Gradual tapering of trunk from base to apex. Done well it creates the effect of a tree in nature, or a large tree.

Koshimizu: Placing the bonsai's pot in a container of water, allowing the tree to absorb water through holes in the pot base. Subirrigation.

Kusamono: A wild grass, alpine plant, etc. grown as a bonsai. In the bonsai world these herbaceous plants serve as indicators for particular seasons or environments. When viewing one in isolation, note the blending of plant and container.

Kyoku: Curve or twist in a trunk or branch; the extent and nature of this curvature.

Kyokuzuke: Bending trunk or branches using wire or tools. Also known as "*moyozuke*."

Kyosei: Wrapping in wire or other material to correct part of a tree deemed unsuitable for a bonsai.

Marukan: Trunk with no scratches or cuts. Trunk with no scarring from wiring or branch cutting.

Mimono: *Zoki* bonsai enjoyed when they are in flower, but especially notable for their superlative viewing value when in fruit.

Mizusui: Parts of a tree currently absorbing water, as opposed to deadwood such as *shari* and *jin*. Also known as the *ikimiki*, or "living trunk."

Mochikomi: Refers to the number of years a tree has been cultivated in a container. When a tree has been cultivated over a long period, and the tree and pot seem almost to fuse, this is admired as "old *mochikomi*."

Mochikuzusu: When a bonsai passes its peak as a "finished" tree and loses its shape.

Moyo: Curves traced by trunk and branches.

Moyogi: Tree with a trunk that curves left to right, forward or back from roots to apex.

Nagare: Flow of the bonsai; the direction in which it is aligned (to right or left) when viewed from the front.

Neagari: Bonsai style in which exposed roots of various sizes thicken over time to become a feature of the tree.

Nearai: Tree, whose roots have grown to fill the pot entirely, that is removed and displayed with roots exposed.

Nebari: The bonsai root system. Good *nebari* consists of stable roots that extend to left and right, gripping the soil firmly. Roots known as "*happone*" that are all the same thickness and stretch out evenly are deemed most attractive.

Netsuranari: Bonsai style that at first glance looks like a *yoseue* (group planting), but consists of trees connected by a single root running along the surface of the soil.

Nikumaki: Cut or scratch in a trunk or branch that has healed and filled in.

Ochi-eda: Branch pointing downward. Can provide visual balance in *binjungi* (literati style) bonsai, but usually considered an *imieda*.

Oikomu: To trim a branch or foliage that has grown too much, detracting from the tree's visual balance. This is often done as a preventive measure.

Omote: Aspect or orientation of a bonsai most suitable for viewing. Also called the *shomen* (front).

Otosu: To sever a surplus branch.

Rakuyoju: General term for trees that send out buds in spring and lose their leaves in fall.

Saku: The state of a bonsai after it has been worked on. Leaving a bonsai in better condition than the previous year is referred to by expressions such as "*saku ga noru*."

Sankan: Bonsai style in which three trunks extend from a single root.

Sashi-eda: Long branch extending from the lower part of the trunk.

Seishi: The task of cutting and bending branches to shape a bonsai in a particular way.

Sentei: Cutting back; pruning.

Shakan: Bonsai modeled on a tree in the wild growing on an unstable coastal or mountain slope, battered by high winds that cause it to grow on a slant.

Shari: Trunk or branch that has rotted as a result of peeling or snapping the bark, exposing the woody center. Often seen in *shohaku* bonsai such as junipers. *Shari* add a charming accent and sense of age, so are often made deliberately using a small blade. *Shari* still retain some living wood, but when the branch dies completely it is known as *jin*.

Shimeru: Cutting back branches and other foliage grown too long, to achieve a more compact, neater overall shape.

Shina-bachi: General term for pots made in China.

Shitakusa: General term for *kusamono* used to highlight the appearance of the main tree in a display, or to add seasonal ambience. Also known as *soe*, or *soekusa*.

Shitate-bachi: Pot used for raising a tree, rather than displaying it. To promote growth, large, well-ventilated pots are preferred.

Shohaku: Evergreen conifer bonsai with year-round foliage. Full of personality and reflecting the ravages of nature in their battered bark, tortured trunks, and tenacious roots, *shohaku* have been favorites since ancient times, and still dominate the bonsai mainstream.

Shoku: A stand designed specifically for bonsai display.

Shomen: See "*omote*."

Shuboku: Main tree in a display. The tree displayed in the most eye-catching position.

Soe: General term for display elements designed to showcase the main tree. Includes *tenpai* (ornaments) and *shitagusa*.

Sokan: Bonsai style in which two trunks grow from a single root. The trunks are trained so one dominates the other in height and girth.

Sozai: Tree "material" for training as a bonsai.

Suiseki: Selecting, displaying, and viewing natural stones.

Tachiagari: Base section from trunk root to first branch.

Takaue: Piling up soil and planting a tree higher than the edges of the pot.

Tenpai: Accessaries used to embellish the theme of a bonsai display.

Uke: General term for a tree, accent plant etc., positioned to counterbalance the trunk or branches of the main tree in a display by accepting its flow and thus accentuating its beauty.

Ura-eda: Branch extending from the back when a tree is viewed from the front.

Uro: Hollow formed when part of a trunk or branch decays and is left bare and bleached.

Uwane: Roots extending horizontally near the surface of the soil. In bonsai it is essential to grow sturdy, healthy *uwane*.

Yakekomi: Part of a trunk that has died and decomposed.

Yaku-eda: The most vital branch for showing off the distinctive form of a tree, its overall mood and ambience.

Yamadori: Taking a tree growing in nature for use as bonsai material. Many famous old bonsai began as *yamadori* trees, however these days taking trees from the wild is prohibited in most areas.

Yoseue: Multiple trees planted in a single container.

Yatsubusa-sho: Dwarf trees with smaller, finer foliage that ordinary varieties. Prized for their ability to reproduce the sensation of a large tree.

Zoki: General term for non-*shohaku* bonsai, e.g., *hamono*, *hanamono*, and *mimono* trees.

（英文版）盆栽・美の極意

The Beauty of Bonsai:
A Guide to Displaying and Viewing Nature's Exquisite Sculpture

2010年9月27日　第1刷発行

著　者　　山本順三

発行者　　廣田浩二

発行所　　講談社インターナショナル株式会社
　　　　　〒112-8652　東京都文京区音羽1-17-14
　　　　　電話　03-3944-6493（編集部）
　　　　　　　　03-3944-6492（マーケティング部・業務部）
　　　　　ホームページ　www.kodansha-intl.com

印刷・製本所　大日本印刷株式会社